GOD'S ANGELS

NATURALLY SUPERNATURAL

Divine Heavenly Helpers

The source of enlightenment is
the Word of God

LEAH LEAMAN

Robb, Thank you so
much for your
support.

Eph 2:6

Blessings & love to
you dear friend.

Blessings,

Leah L.

Published in the USA by Xtreme Glory Ministries
In association with Two Swords Publishing.

Contact information:
Email: leahleaman67@gmail.com
www.xtremeglory.co.uk
www.xtremeglory.net

Scripture quotation marked "AMPC" are taken from the Amplified Classic Bible.
Scripture quotation marked "MSG" are taken from the Message Bible.
Scripture quotation marked "KGV" are taken from the King James Version.
Scripture quotation marked "NIV" are taken from the New International Version.
Scripture quotation marked "TLB" are taken from The Living Bible.
Scripture quotation marked "AKJV" are taken from American King James Version.
Scripture quotation marked "NKJV" are taken from New King James Version.
Scripture quotation marked "TPT" are taken from The Passion Translation.
Scripture quotation marked "NASB" are taken from New American Standard Bible.
Scripture quotation marked "MEV" are taken from Modern English Version.
Scripture quotation marked "GNT" are taken from Good News Translation.
Scripture quotation marked "AMP" are taken from the Amplified Version.

Printed in the United States of America

ISBN: 978-1732678590

1.20

DEDICATION

To my amazing husband, Don, who has stood with
me on this journey allowing me time and space to
follow my heart. Thank you for all of your help,
encouragement and support on this adventure.
You are my best friend and collaborator!

To my sons, Logan and Mitchell, you are my greatest
treasure and I am so proud of you both.
You are a voice to a generation!

Thank you to my parents for their ceaseless love,
prayers, and incredible faith!

CONTENTS

ACKNOWLEDGMENTS

Firstly, Thank You Father in Heaven for
stirring this vision within me and enabling
me to put this book together.

Thank you to Two Swords Publishing for making
this an easy process—flowing from the pages of my
manuscript into a book available for others to read.
Really appreciate all your help and it was truly a
pleasure to work with you on this project

Thank you to Michele Bliss for being a
beta reader for GOD'S ANGELS. I am
grateful for you and our friendship.

Thank you also to my husband Don for
also being a beta reader. Willing to read
and correct this book tirelessly. Love You.

Thank you Mum for all your support and prayer
through the writing of GOD'S ANGELS.
I appreciate and love you!

Thanks also to all my friends who are so
supportive of me on this journey! Your support,
encouragement, and love mean the world to me.

INTRODUCTION

My hope and prayer in writing this book is to help demystify angels. Within these pages I will share scriptures from the Bible to help bring a greater revelation regarding the Angelic Realm and its existence.

This book is meant to be informative to all who read it and hopefully inspiring as you learn from scripture that God's holy angels are divine heavenly helpers and are assigned and commissioned by God to aid and assist us.

For He shall give His angels charge over you,
to keep you in all your ways.
Psalm 91:11 (AMPC)

1

1

THE ANGELIC REALM IS REAL

Without question, the Angelic Realm is real, yet many still refuse to believe in it. Even within the Christian community many are skeptical.

There seems to be a fear factor surrounding the subject of angels that if you mention or discuss them in detail you are worshipping them. Categorically, that is absolutely not the case! If I mention or discuss my husband, children, or even my car, or a restaurant, does that mean I am worshipping them? Again, I say no. I am sharing with you what they are doing, how they are doing, or what they are like. For example, if I like a car, how it performs and so forth, I am simply sharing my opinions and/or facts that provide you information about the vehicle and how I feel.

In most cases, ignorance is to blame when it comes to talking about angels. People are not armed with the full, or even the correct, information from the Word of God. The Bible reveals to us the facts of angels, what angels are, what angels do, and the powerful impact they have or can have on our lives. What the

Bible does not say is, "Thou must not talk about angels".

So, as you turn each page, I pray you gain Biblical understanding and wisdom on the subject! As we open up the Word of God, you will discover that angelic encounters flow from the pages of God's Word. Jesus Christ Himself spoke often about angels. He referred to them in teachings and also received ministry from angels. So, the fact that Jesus believed should be our acid test as Christians.

I want us to have sound Biblical truth concerning the hosts of Heaven and their significance today, both in our lives and in the body of the Church. The Scripture declares in:

Hosea 4:6 (AMPC) - *My people are destroyed through lack of knowledge...*

This is a time to be well-informed and knowledgeable regarding the supernatural realm. Gaining knowledge regarding the multitude of Heavenly Hosts that are at work in heaven, on earth, and in each one of our lives.

And indeed learn, angels have various ranking positions they have been assigned to and operate in. It's also for us to gain understanding of the angelic assistance we have available for us today.

Throughout the Bible, angel assistance is mentioned in so many passages, yet this subject seems to be off limits so much as a whole. I want to bring clarity of how important the angelic realm is in our lives today and how they can function on our behalf.

2

EXPLORE THE ORIGIN OF ANGELS

Some wonder and question what is the origin of the angels mentioned throughout the Bible? Who designed and formed them into being? Why do they exist? Or, do they even exist at all? We are going to explore multiple Biblical passages to help you comprehend the existence of these Heavenly Spirit Beings.

Angels are not relegated to just a few books in the Bible. They are found in 34 of the 66 books. That means angels are mentioned in over half of all the books of the Bible. That's a pretty big deal! Angels are also mentioned in both the first book of the Bible, the book of Genesis, and the last book of the Bible, the book of Revelation.

There are 273 references to angels in the Bible:
- 108 times in the Old Testament of the Bible.
- 165 times in the New Testament of the Bible.

In Genesis 1:1 (AMPC) – We read that Almighty God is bringing all creation into being, BOTH in heaven and on earth. Throughout chapter's one and two in Genesis we see that God spoke and the whole universe came into existence. God repeatedly said, *"Let there be"...* and creation immediately appeared from the invisible realm into the visible.

In another portion of the Bible, in Colossians 1:16-17 (KJV), it says – *For by Him were all things created, that are in heaven, and that are in earth, visible and invisible, whether they be thrones, or dominions, or principalities, or powers; all things were created by Him and for Him. And He is before all things, and by Him all things consist.*

The Message Bible reads the same verse of Colossians 1:16-17 like this - *For everything, absolutely everything, above and below, visible and invisible, rank after rank, after rank of angels - everything got started in Him and finds its purpose in Him. He was there before any of it came into existence and holds it all together right up to this moment. And when it comes to the Church, He organizes and holds it together, like a head does a body.*

It is showing us in these verses that God made everything (both visible and invisible), in heaven and on earth, and when He looked at everything He had made He said it was good and it was 100% approved. Genesis 1:31 (AMPC) says - *And God saw everything He had made, and behold, it was very good [suitable, pleasant] and He approved it completely...*

We believe the Bible is irrefutable, and as you prayerfully study the Word of God you will discover the realm of the spirit is a fact! Our Christianity is based on God, Jesus, and the Holy Spirit, all of which are invisible to the naked eye. We cannot see them yet we believe they are real. We believe by faith. That is what faith is! It is complete trust and confidence in someone or something we cannot see.

Hebrews 11:3 (NIV) reads – *By faith we understand that the universe was formed at God's command, so that what is seen was not made out of what was visible.*

(AMPC) same verse reads like this – *By faith we understand that the worlds [during the successive ages] were framed (fashioned, put in order and equipped for their intended purpose) by the word of God, so that what we see was not made out of things, which are visible.*

There is such a range of life forms so, too, here on earth, from man all the way down to a flea, all of which God created. In the heavenly (angelic realm) there exists a higher level of life, which God also created.

Between God and us there are millions of different spiritual beings at many different levels. We can see from man, going all the way down to a flea, how it works in the visible (natural) realm. So why then, is it so difficult to believe the same applies in the invisible (supernatural) realm, where God dwells? This is where many different types of angels do what they were called and created to do!

We see God's reality and goodness manifest in so many ways: through the working of miracles, signs and wonders, showing us His glory flowing from the invisible realm into the natural, and His power from the unseen into the seen. Angelic helpers are often at work here and we don't even know it. They co-labor between heaven and earth conducting countless activities. It tells us in John 5:4 (AMPC) - *For an angel of the Lord went down at appointed seasons into the pool and moved and stirred up the water; whoever then first, after the stirring up of the water, stepped in was cured of whatever disease with which he was afflicted.*

Angels are commissioned by God to aid and assist us as we yield to and follow Him. Psalm 91:11 (AMPC) reads – *For He will give His angels [special] charge over you to accompany and defend and preserve you in all your ways [of obedience and service].* They are on a divine mission to assist and protect us as children of God, as it states in this verse.

3

HEAVENLY HOSTS AT WORK

Angels are at work every day in our lives. They hold various positions both in heaven and on earth, and we can gain greater understanding of their assignments and tasks as we read through the Bible.

The expression and explicit teaching of scripture shows us that between man and God, there is so much activity going on in the supernatural realm with spiritual beings that we cannot see with our own natural (physical) eyes. However, around us is a spiritual world far more populous than earth, far more powerful than earth, and far more resourceful than our own visible world. If we could pull back the curtain into the spiritual world we would probably faint, get up, and then faint again.

We see the very instance of this in the second book of Kings (on the following page). Elisha's servant panicked, as he could not see what Elisha was seeing in the invisible realm, until Elisha prayed for the Lord to open up his servant's eyes so that he also would be able to see what Elisha was seeing.

> 2 Kings 6:14-17 (MSG) – *Then he [the Syrian king]*
> *dispatched horses and chariots, an impressive fighting*
> *force. They came by night and surrounded the city. Early*
> *in the morning a servant of the Holy Man got up and*
> *went out. Surprise! Horses and chariots surrounding the*
> *city! The young man exclaimed, "Oh, master! What*
> *should we do?" He said, "Don't worry about it there are*
> *more on our side than on their side." Then Elisha*
> *prayed, "O God, open his eyes and let him see." The eyes*
> *of the young man were opened and he saw. A wonder!*
> *The whole mountainside full of horses and chariots of fire*
> *surrounding Elisha!*

Around us are angelic hosts and spirits, both good and evil, and they are always moving in our midst. They pass from place to place instantly, with lightning speed and noiseless movement, and inhabit the space of the air all around us! Unlike man, they are not limited by physical and natural conditions. Angels are spirits. They are spiritual beings that can appear or disappear at will and, as I mentioned earlier, they travel at unimaginable speed without the use of natural means!

Though purely spirits, they have the power to assume human form making their presence visible to our senses. In other words angels, from time to time, may transform themselves into a human form so we can actually see them. This does not mean they become human, but they can take on human form to help us associate with them. Here are some examples:

Genesis 19:1 (AMPC) – *It was evening when the two angels came to Sodom's [city] gate. Seeing them, Lot rose up to meet them...*

Luke 22:43 (AMPC) – *And there appeared to Him an angel from heaven, strengthening Him in spirit.*

Acts 27:23 (AMPC) – *For this [very night] stood by my side an angel of the God to Whom I belong and serve and worship...*

Hebrews 13:2 (TLB) – *Don't forget to be kind to strangers, for some who have done this have entertained angels without realizing it!*

Matthew 28:2-5 (AMPC) – *And behold, there was a great earthquake, for an angel of the Lord descended from heaven and came and rolled the boulder back and sat upon it. His appearance was like lightning and his garments as white as snow. And those keeping guard were frightened at the sight of him and they were agitated and they trembled and became like dead men. But the angel said to the women, "Do not be alarmed and frightened, for I know that you are looking for Jesus, Who was crucified. He is not here: He had risen as He said [He would do]"...*

4

INNUMERABLE ANGELS

Looking back to Genesis, and in the beginning, it also mentions in Genesis 2:1 (AMPC) - *Thus the heavens and the earth were finished, and all the host of them.*

The hosts of heaven, as we will discover and read about from the Bible, are so vast and too innumerable to number. The word "host" in Hebrew means "armies". So when we read scripture and it refers to God as, "The Lord of hosts", it basically means "He is Lord of the heavenly armies".

By all accounts, the angelic hosts are enormous! Hebrews 12:22 (AKJV) mentions, *an innumerable company of angels.* The Amplified Bible refers in the same verse as, *countless multitudes of angels.* Also, they are often referred to many times as myriads of angels, to mean countless or extremely great in number! Only God himself knows the exact number of angels that exist for sure, as He created each of them and also commissioned each one of them with tasks to perform. As God is omniscient [all-knowing], He knew how many He needed to perform the work that

He knew needed to be fulfilled.

Revelation 5:11-12 (AMPC) - *Then I looked, and I heard the voices of many angels on every side of the throne and of the living creatures and the elders, and they numbered ten thousand times ten thousand and thousands of thousands.*

So by that calculation, that totals over one hundred million angels. I think they are presented to us as uncountable at times because our mind cannot grasp the magnitude of their numerical quantity. I pray our minds get flooded with revelatory light so that we become enlightened as we gaze into the realm of wonder and know that it is more real than life itself.

In the book of Psalms, King David wrote, Psalm 68:17 (KJV) - *The chariots of God are twenty thousand, even thousands of angels: the Lord is among them, as in Sinai, in the holy place.*

Scripture makes it clear that God wants us to be aware of the existence of the angelic hosts, and the nature of their activity. They play an important role in heaven and here on earth!

Angels also come in many different forms, which God designed from the book of Genesis. It is important to see and understand that angels were created just like we were, by a divine supernatural act of God and they are as real as we are! Angels are not the same as us, but like us. They are part of the heavenly hosts from a realm far greater than this

16

world and they are representatives of heaven and are just as real as we are. Albeit, they are invisible for the most part and operate in that arena.

5

ARMY RANKS OF THE ANGELIC

Scripture shows us angels have diverse and specific assignments. The Bible talks about different positions of hierarchy within the angelic realm, which God designed in the book of Genesis. The Message version of the Bible uses the word rank, which again shows a chain of command and a system of order depending on their divine mandate, status, and ministry.

Colossians 1:16-17 (MSG) - *For everything, absolutely everything, above and below, visible and invisible, rank after rank, after rank of angels- everything got started in Him and finds its purpose in Him. He was there before any of it came into existence and holds it all together right up to this moment. And when it comes to the Church, He organizes and holds it together, like a head does a body.*

Colossians 1:16-17 (KJV) – *For by Him were all things created, that are in heaven, and that are in earth, visible and invisible, whether they be thrones, or dominions, or principalities, or powers; all things were created by Him and For Him. And He is before all things, and by Him all things consist.*

Genesis 2:1 (AMPC) – *Thus the heavens and the earth were finished, and all the host of them.*

I mentioned this earlier and here it is again, the word "host" in Hebrew means "armies", so when we read scripture and it refers to God as, "The Lord of hosts", it means "He is Lord of the heavenly armies".

Revelation 19:14 (AMPC) mentions - *And the troops of heaven, clothed in fine linen, dazzling and clean, followed Him on white horses.*

(KJV) reads – *And the armies, which were in heaven, followed Him upon white horses, clothed in fine linen, white and clean.*

In the book of Matthew, Jesus asked the question to those who were with Him at that time, Mathew 26:53 (AMPC) - *Do you suppose that I cannot appeal to My Father, and He will immediately provide Me with more than twelve legions [more than 80,000] of angels?*

Notice the usage of the word "legion", which Jesus used, again showing a chain of command in operation. A legion of men in Roman army terms varied at different times. But in the time of Christ, it seems to have consisted of roughly 6,826 men, both foot soldiers and horsemen. So that multiplied by 12 takes it to nearly 82,000 angels.

Dwelling on and looking deeper into reference details like these gives us a greater perspective on the importance of these details. So many times we run over scripture without really taking time to think of the magnitude of what Jesus is declaring. It is particularly evident in Matthew 26:53 (AMPC) that, *"If I appeal to My Father, He will immediately provide angelic assistance to help Me"*...

It is good information to know, realize and understand that angels are a highly organized hierarchy over which Christ sovereignly reigns. The dictionary definition of the word "information" is, "Facts provided or learned about something or someone." Information brings clarification - to make clear an idea, or statement, to free (the mind's intelligence) from confusion and to revive.

So I pray the information and truth given through this book will break all confusion and bring a newfound freedom, clarity, understanding and revelation in this subject area.

6

ANGELS DON'T RECEIVE WORSHIP

We are not to worship angels. Our source for understanding angels is the Word of God. We must never forget that! One of the first commandments in Exodus 20:3-5 (NKJV) – *You shall have no other gods before Me. You shall not make for yourself a carved image, any likeness of anything that is in heaven above, or that is in the earth beneath, or that is in the water under the earth, you shall not bow down to them or serve them. For I the Lord your God am a jealous God…*

This is telling us that if we worship angels we are violating His commandment. It teaches and instructs us in the Bible the worship of angels is something that is condemned. Only God is to be worshipped – God and Him alone. God means self-existent one!

Angels are created beings. Therefore, they depend on God to exist. The word create is a Hebrew word "Bara", which means "Only God can"… [Create]. It is God's creative activity that created angels, and angels always direct worship to where it belongs, which is to God alone who created heaven and earth.

Nehemiah 9:5-6 (MSG) - *Blessed be your glorious name, exalted above all blessing and praise! You're the one, God, you alone; You made the heavens, the heavens of heavens, and all the angels; The earth and everything on it, the seas and everything in them. You keep them all alive; heaven's angels worship you.*

Heavenly angels worship God and will not allow you to worship them. Their focus always points to the sovereignty of the King of kings and the Lords of lords, and they are pure, purposeful beings, greater in power and might than us mortals! It also shows us in these verses that angels dare not bring abusive condemnation before the Lord regarding a situation or us.

2 Peter 2:10-11 (NKJV) says - ... *and especially those who walk according to the flesh in the lust of uncleanness and despise authority. They are presumptuous and self-willed. They are not afraid to speak evil of dignitaries, whereas angels, who are greater in power and might do not bring reviling accusation against them before the Lord.*

Jude 1:9 (AMPC) - *But [even] when the Archangel Michael, contending with the devil, judicially argued (disputed) about the body of Moses, he dared not*

*[presume to] bring an abusive condemnation against him,
but [simply said], the Lord rebuke you.*

It also shows us in these next verses not to be misled into error by false teachers into angel worship. Colossians 2:18 (AMPC) - *Let no one defraud you by acting as an umpire and declaring you unworthy and disqualifying you for the prize, insisting on self-abasement and worship of angels, taking his stand on visions [he claims] he has seen, vainly puffed up by his sensuous notions and inflated by his unspiritual thoughts and fleshly conceit.*

Here are two separate incidents when John the Apostle was rebuked when he initially bowed down to worship an angel in the book of Revelation 22:8-9 (AMPC) *...I fell prostrate before the feet of the messenger [angel] who showed them to me, to worship him. But he said to me, Refrain! [You must not do that!] I am [only] a fellow servant along with yourself and with your brethren the prophets and with those who are mindful of and practice [the truths contained in] the messages of this book. WORSHIP GOD!*

Then in Revelation 19:10 (AMPC) - *Then I fell prostrate at his feet to worship [to pay divine honor] to him, but he [restrained me] and said, Refrain! [You must not do that!] I am only another servant with you and your brethren...*

Again, this is so important for us to remember, like us, angels were created by an act of God. He created everything, and since He created everything, it saddens Him when we bow down to the things that He created rather than realizing the Creator Himself exists.

Some religions bow down to and worship animals, snakes, carved objects of wood, stone or gold. Some adore, pray and even kiss concrete. Some worship people, money, a lifestyle and other things rather than the Creator of all these things. So angels, being created just like us, are not to be worshipped.

To further clarify - Exodus 20:3-5 (NKJV) - *You shall have no other gods before Me. You shall not make for yourself a carved image, any likeness of anything that is in heaven above, or that is in the earth beneath, or that is in the water under the earth, you shall not bow down to them or serve them. For I the Lord your God Am a jealous God...*

He is the only one we worship. Nehemiah 9:5-6 (MSG) - *Blessed be your glorious name, exalted above all blessing and praise! You're the one, God, you alone; You made the heavens, the heavens of heavens, and all the angels; The earth and everything on it, the seas and everything in them. You keep them all alive; heavens angels worship you.*

Our unified and direct purpose is to worship and adore God alone. Not because it is a commandment [though it is] or an instruction [though it is], but out of our absolute passion, desire and love for Him, because He first loved us. Before Him, we should stand in awe and wonder at His indescribable beauty that is altogether glorious and defies imagination and that no metaphor or words in any earthly language can describe or comprehend.

In Peter, it mentions angels are subject to Christ, subservient to Him. Subservient means prepared to obey others unquestioningly. 1 Peter 3:22 (AMPC) -

[And He] has now entered into heaven and is at the right hand of God with [all] angels and authorities and powers made subservient to Him.

7

NO NEW ANGELS

All angels [hosts] were created at one time. No new angels are being added to the number. Heaven and earth were complete in the beginning and the work was complete and finished as it states in this verse in Genesis.

It says in Genesis 2:1 (AMPC) - *Thus the heavens and the earth were finished, and all the host of them.*

Angels are not subject to death or any form of extinction; they are immortal therefore they do not decrease in number. Luke 20:35-36 (TPT) – *But those who are worthy of the resurrection from the dead into glory become immortal, like the angels, who never die nor marry.*

Amplified Classic version puts it like this - *Neither can they die any more: for they are equal unto angels; and are the children of God, being the children of the resurrection.*

Angels are spirit beings, meaning they are eternal beings rather than human beings with physical bodies like us! Our natural body dies, but our spirits can go to either one of two places – Heaven or Hell.

Hebrews 1:14 (AMPC) - *Are not the angels all ministering spirits [servants] sent out in the service [of God for the assistance] of those who are to inherit salvation.*

Psalm 104: 4 (AMPC) - *Who makes winds His messengers, flames of fire His ministers.*

Hebrews 1:7 (AMPC) - *Referring to the angels He says, [God] Who makes His angels winds and His ministering servants flames of fire.*

8

MINISTERING SPIRITS

Angels are heavenly spirit beings created by God for His purposes. The word angel in Greek [angelos] means "messenger". They are God's divine/heavenly messengers that He uses to fulfill His will both in heaven and on earth.

> Hebrews 1:14 (AMPC) - *Are not the angels all ministering spirits [servants] sent out in the service [of God for the assistance] of those who are to inherit salvation.*

The word "minister" in Greek is [diakonia], referring to their "serviceable labor, assistance." So, angels are ministering spirits, or heavenly assistants, who are continually active! Thus, it is important to realize the function of angels in our life here and now, and that God uses them to assist us as they execute God's purpose. They are personal heavenly assistants to God and attend to all that is required of them.

LEAH LEAMAN

9

WHAT ANGELS DO

Psalm 103:20-21 (NASB) - *Bless the Lord, you His angels, mighty in strength, who perform His word, obeying the voice of His word. Bless the Lord, all you His hosts, you who serve Him, doing His will.*

This verse reveals the purposes and attributes of angels. They worship and praise the Lord Jesus Christ. They are mighty in strength. They do His word. They obey the voice of His word. They serve Him. They do His will.

First as mentioned in Psalm 103:20 (AMPC) - *The angels of God blessing Him,* we can only imagine the scene of such devotion and awe exhibited by such glorious beings as they extol His Holy Name. They worship the Lord of Hosts day and night, night and day 24-7! All heaven declares in Revelation 4:11 (AMPC) - *Worthy are You, our Lord and God, to receive the glory and the honor and dominion, for You created all things; by Your will they were [brought into being] and were created.*

Second, as mentioned in the same verse is that they

are mighty in strength. It also reveals this in 2 Thessalonians, 1:7 (AMPC) - *as His mighty angels...* In 2 Peter 2: 11 (AMPC) - *Whereas [even] angels, superior in might and power...*

Angels are strong and powerful beings that God uses for many different tasks. There is no possible way to number all the diverse actions and activities that take place in the angelic realm.

Third, it says angels perform His word. Whatever God asks the angels to do, they perform it, like delivering this message to Joseph. Reading in Matthew 1:20 (AMPC) - *But as he was thinking this over, behold, an angel of the Lord appeared to him in a dream, saying, Joseph, do not be afraid to take Mary as your wife...*

That is why angels are called Messengers; they deliver messages of what God wants to do in our lives. Another message that was delivered to Zachariah in Luke 1:13 (AMPC) - *But the angel said to him. Do not be afraid Zachariah, because your petition was heard, and your wife Elizabeth will bear you a son...* There are many other verses that can also be found regarding angels delivering messages.

And last, it mentions angels obey the voice of His word. Meaning, each time we speak God's Word we are also giving voice to His Word!

When angels hear His word (including us reading, praying or declaring God's Word out loud), they respond. We are mobilizing angels when we speak the Word of God.

Let me be clear, WE DO NOT pray to the angels. That is never to be the case. We pray to God. The angels listen to our words and go into action as they hear God's Word being given a voice and spoken.

In Psalm 103:20 (AMPC) the word used is … *"hearkening" to the voice of His word.* To hearken means, "to listen for, to pay close attention to, and to hear and do".

As stated earlier, angels are listening and paying close attention for the voice of God's Word to be spoken, they hear and respond to it. On the other hand, when we speak negative words of doubt and unbelief we take the angels out of the picture.

In the presence of those negative words, angels have no choice but to bow their heads, cross their arms and wait. Proverbs 18:20-21 (AMPC) - *A man's [moral] self shall be filled with the fruit of his mouth; and with the consequence of his words he must be satisfied [whether good or evil]. Death and life are in the power of the tongue, and they who indulge in it [for death or life].* The angels want you to speak life and the Word of God and do it consistently enough for them to get provision to you.

Which brings us to the second part of Psalm 103:21 (AMPC) - it mentions *"Bless the Lord all you His hosts, you who serve Him, doing His will."*

Angels are on assignments; they are beings of action and they have a mission and mandate to fulfill. They do the will of God; what is acceptable to him and well-pleasing in His sight and indeed they bear a leading part in giving praise and glory to God.

10

TYPES OF ANGELS

(A) ARCHANGELS

Archangels are the top rank of the heavenly hosts. Prior to Lucifer's fall, there were three archangels. Now there are only two, Michael and Gabriel.

The fallen angel named Lucifer, which means, "bearer of light" or, "morning star," now refers to his former splendor. See Isaiah 14:12-15 (AMPC) - *How have you fallen from heaven, O light-bringer and daystar, son of the morning! How you have been cut down to the ground, you who weakened and laid low the nations [O blasphemous, satanic king of Babylon!] And you said in your heart, I will ascend to heaven; I will exalt my throne above the stars of God; I will sit upon the mount of assembly in the uttermost north. I will ascend above the heights of the clouds; I will make myself like the Most High. Yet you shall be brought down to Sheol (Hades), to the innermost recesses of the pit (the region of the dead).*

The word archangel is mentioned in two passages of the Bible. It is a Greek word, "archaggelos" meaning a ruler, a superior angel, an archangel.

1 Thessalonians 4:16 (AMPC) - *For the Lord Himself will descend from heaven with a loud cry of summons, with the shout of an archangel, and with the blast of the trumpet of God...*

Jude 1:9 (AMPC) - *But when [even] the archangel Michael, contending with the devil, judicially argued (disputed) about the body of Moses...*

Michael means – "Who is like God."

Gabriel means – "The mighty one of God."

We find Michael is mentioned by name on four different instances in the Bible, both in the Old Testament and in the New Testament. Michael is a mighty warring angel, one of the chief celestial princes and a national guardian angel.

Daniel 10:13 (AMPC) reads - *... Then Michael, one of the chief [of the celestial] princes, came to help me, for I remained there with the kings of Persia.* Also, Daniel 10:21 (AMPC) – *...There is no one who holds with me and strengthens himself against these [hostile spirit forces] except Michael, your prince [national guardian angel].*

Again in Daniel 12:1 (AMPC) - *And at that time [of the end] Michael shall arise, the great [angelic] prince who defends and has charge of your [Daniel's] people...*

On reading the chapters that contain these verses, it helps us discover the important assignment Michael has and is in charge of, standing up for Israel during the time of tribulation.

In the book of Thessalonians, Paul, the writer of this book gives encouragement to believers and pays particular attention to the hope of Christ's return. It shows us here that a mighty archangel is going to "shout" as the Lord descends from heaven, on His return. So that is one of the duties we find that an archangel will be tasked. It reads in 1 Thessalonians 4:16 (AMPC) - *For the Lord Himself will descend from heaven with a loud cry of summons, with the shout of an archangel, and with the blast of the trumpet of God...*

Now to learn about the other mighty archangel named Gabriel. Remember, his name means "the mighty one of God". Gabriel is mentioned in both the Old and New Testament of the Bible and is a mighty archangel of God who is identified as a divine messenger who delivers important prophetic messages to servants of God, and is used to release understanding (revelation) of dreams and visions. We see this in chapter 8 of the book of Daniel where Gabriel explains the visions Daniel had.

The first mention of Gabriel in the Bible is in an appearance to the prophet Daniel. In this verse, Gabriel is summoned to show Daniel the meaning of a vision he had received regarding the kings of Media, Persia, and Greece (Daniel 8:15-26). In these verses, we discover Gabriel had the appearance of a man and spoke to Daniel, touched Daniel, and caused him to understand a vision he had seen. Gabriel is mentioned by name here in Daniel 8:16 (AMPC) - ...*Gabriel make this man [Daniel] understand the vision.*

> Daniel 9:21-22 (AMPC) - *Yes, while I was speaking in prayer, the man Gabriel, whom I had seen in the former vision, being caused to fly swiftly, came near to me and touched me about the time of the evening sacrifice. He instructed me and made me understand; he talked with me and said, Daniel, I am now come forth to give you skill and wisdom and understanding.*

One of Gabriel's main missions is to release insight and understanding of what God is saying and showing in visions. He is extremely active in the revelatory arena and causes understanding to take place as well as delivering news and insight into future events.

Gabriel is mentioned again communicating with Zachariah in the book of Luke. Zachariah was disputing with the archangel Gabriel that if he could be sure of what he was hearing! Luke 1:19 (AMPC) - *And the angel replied to him, I am Gabriel, I stand in the [very] presence of God, and I have been sent to talk to you and to bring you this good news.*

Gabriel was announcing to Zachariah and making sure that Zachariah knew who he was and Gabriel was also proclaiming his close proximity and intimate access with God, declaring that he stood in the very presence of God!

Gabriel was trying to convey to Zachariah if you really know who I am, and where I stand, you would never question me. So here is a message from God for you! Be sure and believe it!!!

Again, we see further down in the same chapter that Gabriel also had the mission to deliver the glorious news announcing the birth of Jesus to Mary. Luke 1:26 (AMPC) - *Now on the sixth month [after that], the angel Gabriel, was sent from God to a town of Galilee named Nazareth...*

Over the next few verses we read of a conversation and discussion back and forth that went on between Gabriel and Mary. Mary was a virgin, having never been married, however she was engaged to Joseph. We follow when Gabriel was talking to Mary in Luke 1:27 (AMPC) - *And he came to her and said, Hail, O favored one [endued with grace]! The Lord is with you! Blessed (favored of God) are you before all other women! And the angel said to her, Do not be afraid, Mary, for you have found grace with God. And listen! You will become pregnant and will give birth to a son, and you shall call His name Jesus. He will be great (eminent) and will be called Son of the Most High; and the Lord God will give to Him the throne of His forefather David. And He will reign over the house of Jacob through the ages; and of His reign there will be no end...*

In verse 34 - Mary said to the angel; in verse 35 – The angel said to Mary; then in verse 36 – *The angel told Mary to listen...* He shared with her news and insight that her cousin called Elizabeth was six months pregnant. Luke 1:36-37 (MSG) reads *"And did you know that your cousin Elizabeth conceived a son, old as she is. Everyone called her barren, and here she is six months*

41

pregnant! Nothing you see is impossible with God."

So a great interaction was taking place here with a mighty angel of God named Gabriel and with Mary, soon to be the mother of Jesus. An important prophetic message was being delivered to Mary and notice the angel also perceived the troubled thoughts and confusion that was going on in her (Mary's) mind and told her not to be afraid! Gabriel tried to reassure and comfort Mary during the delivery of this message as she tried to process the word that was being brought to her.

It also tells us in the book of Matthew, as Joseph (Mary's fiancé) was thinking and mulling this whole scenario over of, "How did this happen", " What should I do", an angel of the Lord appeared to him in a dream, saying in Matthew 1:20 (AMPC) – *Joseph descendant of David, do not be afraid to take Mary [as] your wife, for that which is conceived in her of (from, out of) the Holy Spirit...* It tells us in verse 24 that Joseph being aroused from his sleep did as the angel of the Lord commanded him and made Mary his wife.

So Joseph also had a very real experience with an angel of the Lord in the form of a dream and as he was questioning the purity of Mary an angel was dispatched to assure and guide Joseph in his way!

Additionally, an angel of the Lord instructed and warned Joseph, this time about the plot of Herod to find and destroy baby Jesus. Matthew 2:13-23 (AMPC) tells us Joseph obeyed the instructions of the angel and took Jesus and Mary to Egypt and he was told to remain there until told otherwise. Years later Joseph had another dream which told him it was good to go, rise and take your family to Israel. Being divinely warned in a dream, he withdrew to the region of Galilee.

It shows us that Gabriel must have been an awesome sight to behold, as the presence of the mighty archangel came to deliver messages, so heavenly brilliant, holy and overwhelming, that when heaven comes near, even in the form of an angel, you can't stand in the very presence of such a glorious being without being overcome with awe and holiness. As mere mortals, when the very atmosphere and the very presence of God fills the location where we are, we just can't stand as the weight of the glory of God enters our natural world and a Holy fear and reverence takes over. The following verses demonstrate this!

In the book of Daniel 8:18 (AMPC) – *Now as he [Gabriel] was speaking with me, I fell stunned and in deep unconsciousness with my face to the ground: but he touched me and set me upright [where I had stood].*

When Gabriel showed up to Zachariah in Luke 1:12, it tells us that Zachariah was troubled and fear took possession of him. Gabriel told him not to be afraid.

In Luke 1:19, it tells us that Gabriel replied to Zachariah's question of, *"How can I be sure of this"* by saying, *"I am Gabriel, I stand in the [very] presence of God, and I have been sent to talk to you and to bring you this good news".*

Angels are mentioned in these very important assignments below:

An angel announces the birth of Jesus Christ in Luke 2:9-14 (AMPC) - *And behold, an angel of the Lord stood by them, and the glory of the Lord flashed and shone all about them, and they were terribly frightened. But the angel of the Lord said to them. Do not be afraid; for I bring you good news of a great joy, which will come to all the people. For to you is born this day in the town of David a Savior, Who is Christ (the Messiah) the Lord!* Jump to verse 13 – *Then suddenly there appeared with the angel an army of the troops of heaven (a heavenly knighthood) praising God and saying Glory to God in the highest [heaven], and on earth peace among men with whom He is well pleased...*

Another is mentioned in Luke when an angel strengthened Christ in the Garden of Gethsemane. Luke 22:43 (AMPC) - *And there appeared to Him an angel from heaven, strengthening Him in spirit.*

Another mention is in the wonderful resurrection of Jesus Christ when an angel rolled the stone away from the front of the tomb where Jesus had been buried. Matthew 28:2-6 (AMPC) - *And behold, there was a great earthquake, for an angel of the Lord descended from heaven and came and rolled the boulder back and sat upon it. His appearance was like lightning and his garments as white as snow. And those keeping guard were so frightened at the sight of him that they were agitated and they trembled and became like dead men. But the angel said to the woman, do not be alarmed and frightened, for I know you are looking for Jesus,*

Who was crucified. He is not here; He has risen, as He said [He would do]. Come see the place where he lay.

An angel freed the apostles from prison in Acts 5:19 (AMPC) - *But during the night an angel of the Lord opened the prison doors and, leading them out, said, Go take your stand in the temple courts and declare to the people the whole doctrine concerning this life (the eternal life which Christ revealed).*

An angel sent Philip to the desert of Gaza to meet the eunuch. It reads in Acts 8:26 (AMPC) - *But an angel of the Lord said to Philip, rise and proceed southward or at midday on the road that runs down to Gaza…*

An angel instructed Cornelius to send for Peter in Acts 10:3 (AMPC) - *About the ninth hour (about 3pm) of the day he saw clearly in a vision an angel of God entering and saying to him, "Cornelius." And he, gazing intently at him, became frightened and said, "What is it Lord?" And the angel said to him, "Your prayers and your [generous] gifts to the poor have come up [as a sacrifice] to God and have been remembered by Him…"*

We find in another portion, where an angel executed wicked Herod for blasphemy in Acts 12:23 (AMPC) - *And at once an angel of the Lord smote him and cut him down, because he did not give God the Glory…*

An angel gives Paul assurance on a sinking ship. Paul speaking here to his shipmates in Acts 27:23 (AMPC) - *For this [very] night there stood by my side an angel of the God to Whom I belong and Whom I serve and worship. And he said do not be frightened Paul! It is necessary for you to stand before Caesar; and behold God has given you all those who are sailing with you. So keep up your courage, men, for I have faith...*

We must never forget that angels are ministering spirits sent forth to aid the heirs of salvation. We find in Hebrews 1:14, if God entrusted them with guidance and care at the birth of Jesus and so forth, they are surely equipped to aid us.

(B) Cherubim

Next we will look at a group of angels revealed to us as Cherubim in the Bible. Cherubim are powerful types of beings so do not be misguided by their name. They are not cute little babies with wings. We find out in scripture they are huge heavenly warriors, mighty and powerful guardians of God. From the very beginning in Genesis we find they were sent to the Garden of Eden to protect and guard the tree of life with flaming swords.

> Genesis 3:24 (AMPC) - *So [God] drove out the man; and He placed at the east of the Garden of Eden the cherubim and a flaming sword which turned everyway, to keep and guard the way to the tree of life.*

So we find here that cherubim angels were sent to the garden as guardians, to protect and guard the tree of life, wielding flaming swords powerfully, to make known there was absolutely no access allowed! This causes such a dramatic vision of these cherubim angels. Again, not cute little babies as often thought!

Cherubim angels are also named in the Bible as living creatures and that comes from the prophet Ezekiel when he recorded, in detail, his encounter in the book of Ezekiel. He said the heavens were opened and I saw visions of God!

What a dramatic vision he had of these cherubim angels, certainly an amazing scene. Ezekiel's vision might seem strange, but it is the wonder of the supernatural realm and the existence thereof. Here is the passage of scripture containing the vision.

Ezekiel 1:4-28 (AMPC) - *As I looked, behold, a stormy wind came out of the north, and a great cloud with a fire enveloping it and flashing continually; a brightness was about it and out of the midst of it there seemed to glow amber metal, out of the midst of the fire. And out of the midst of it came the likeness of four living creatures [or cherubim]. And this was their appearance: they had the likeness of a man, but each one had four faces and each one had four wings. And their legs were straight legs, and the sole of their feet was like the sole of a calf's foot, and they sparkled like burnished bronze. And they had the hands of a man under their wings on their four sides. And the four of them had their faces and their wings thus: Their wings touched one another; they turned not when they went but went every one straight forward As for the likeness of their faces, they each had the face of a man [in front], and each had the face of a lion on the right side and the face of an ox on the left side; the four*

*also had the face of an eagle [at the back of their heads].
Such were their faces. And their wings were stretched out
upward [each creature had four wings]; two wings of each
one were touching the [adjacent] wing of the creatures on
either side of it, and [the remaining] two wings of each
creature covered its body. And they went every one
straight forward; wherever the spirit would go, they went,
and they turned not when they went. In the midst of the
living creatures there was what looked like burning coals
of fire, like torches moving to and fro among the living
creatures; the fire was bright and out of the fire went forth
lightning. And the living creatures darted back and forth
like a flash of lightning. Now as I was still looking at the
living creatures, I saw one wheel upon the ground beside
each of the living creatures with its four faces. As to the
appearance of the wheels and their construction: in
appearance they gleamed like chrysolite; and the four were
formed alike, and their construction work was as it were
a wheel within a wheel. When they went, they went in one
of their four directions without turning [for they were faced
that way]. As for their rims, they were so high that they
were dreadful, and the four had their rims full of eyes
round about. And when the living creatures went, the
wheels went beside them; and when the living creatures
were lifted up from the earth, the wheels were lifted up.
Wherever the spirit went, the creatures went and the
wheels rose along with them, for the spirit or life of the*

[four living creatures acting as one] living creature was in the wheels. When those went, these went; and when those stood, these stood; and when those were lifted up from the earth, the wheels were lifted up high beside them, for the spirit or life of the [combined] living creature was in the wheels. Over the head of the [combined] living creature there was the likeness of a firmament, looking like the terrible and awesome [dazzling of shining] crystal or ice stretched across the expanse of sky over their heads. And under the firmament their wings were stretched out straight, one toward another. Every living creature had two wings, which covered its body on this side, and two, which covered it on that side. And when they went, I heard the sound of their wings like the noise of great waters, like the voice of the Almighty, the sound of tumult like the noise of a host. When they stood, they let down their wings. And there was a voice above the firmament that was over their heads; when they stood, they let down their wings. And above the firmament that was over their heads was the likeness of a throne in appearance like a sapphire stone, and seated above the likeness of a throne was a likeness with the appearance of a Man. From what had the appearance of His waist upward, I saw a luster as it were glowing metal with the appearance of fire enclosed round about within it; and from the appearance of His waist downward, I saw as it were the appearance of fire, and there was brightness [of a

halo] round about Him. Like the appearance of the bow that is in the cloud on the day of rain, so was the appearance of the brightness round about. This was the appearance of the likeness of the glory of the Lord. And when I saw it, I fell upon my face and I heard a voice of One speaking.

What an amazing scene. Here we have a detailed description of cherubim. Ezekiel describes each cherub as having four faces, yet the likeness of a man.

The face in front is a man.

The face on the right is a lion.

The face on the left is an ox.

The face on the back is an eagle.

The four faces of these living creatures are symbolic of the four representations of Jesus as given in the first four books of the New Testament in the Bible.

Matthew represents Him as the King – the lion.

Mark portrays Him as the Servant – the ox.

Luke emphasizes His humanity – the man.

John proclaims foremost His deity – the eagle.

What an astounding sight to behold and process. We see from this the cherubim have two pairs of wings each. It also informs us that two wings of each cherubim were touching the adjacent wings of the cherubim on either side, so with their outstretched wings from each one touching those of the three remaining companions wings, they form a square, and the other pair of wings is used to cover the body, hence four wings in total.

Ezekiel 1:24 (MSG) reads like this - *Over the heads of the living creatures was something like a dome, shimmering like a sky full of cut glass, vaulted over their heads. Under the dome one set of wings was extended toward the others, with another set of wings covering their bodies. When they moved I heard their wings-it was like the roar of a great waterfall, like the voice of the strong God, like the noise of a battlefield. When they stopped, they folded their wings.*

We can pull out from some of the verses the tremendous volume of sound being created by the movement of their wings and the intensity of the noise being released by their actions.

Ezekiel 10:5 (AMPC) - *And the sound of the wings of the cherubim was heard even to the outer court, like the voice of God Almighty when He speaks.*

Ezekiel 3:13 (AMPC) - *I heard the noise of the wings of the living creatures as they touched and joined each one the other [its sister wing], and I heard the noise of the wheels beside them and the noise of a great rushing.*

Now it tells us that the cherubim have straight legs,

but their feet are cloven like a calf's foot and they shine like burnished brass and they also have [four human hands located under each wing].

Ezekiel 1:7-8 (AMPC) - *And their legs were straight legs, and the sole of their feet was like the sole of a calf's foot, and they sparkled like burnished bronze. And they had the hands of a man under their wings on their four sides...*

When the cherubim went anywhere, they went in any of the four directions in which their four individual faces were turned: they did not turn as they moved but would go in a straight line, in any of the four ways their faces looked.

Ezekiel 10:11 (TLB) - *...the angels could go straight forward in each of four directions; they did not turn when they changed direction but could go in any of the four ways their faces looked.*

How fascinating to behold these beings of glory, these awesome creatures that are built to defend and protect the very presence and holiness of God. It also mentions in Ezekiel 1:14, that they can move at a phenomenal rate, darting back and forth like a flash of lightning. As I mentioned earlier, when cherubim angels moved (Ezekiel 1:24), the sound of their wings was like a noise of great waters, like the voice of the Almighty.

As we enter into the realm of God, we begin to

perceive how His kingdom is and operates! Not quite the cute little cherubs that are depicted now, are they! The Word of God is always our compass and as we take time to study and meditate on these truths from the Word of God, it causes illumination to take place. As we pursue greater revelation and knowledge of the invisible realm, the Bible then helps us to build pictures by the descriptive text, which gives us a visual aid in our mind, into the realm and dimension of God. It creates and paints a picture for us to be able to grasp that the invisible realm exists, what it looks like, it is in operation right now, and that it coincides with our natural realm of gravity.

When God was directing the building of the tabernacle in Exodus 25, He told Moses to carve two golden cherubim and place them at either end of the lid of the Ark of the Covenant, the mercy seat in the Holy of Holies.

Exodus 25:18 (AMPC) - *And you shall make two cherubim; (winged angelic figures) of (solid) hammered gold on the two ends of the mercy seat... Verse 22 ...There I will meet with you and, from between the two cherubim that are upon the ark of the Testimony. I will speak intimately with you...*

Their role is to guard God's Holy Domain and presence from any sin and corruption as mighty and powerful guardians of God. The author of Hebrews calls the cherubim symbols of God's glory. Hebrews 9:5 (AMPC) – *Above [the ark] and overshadowing the mercy seat were the representations of the cherubim [winged creatures which were the symbols] of glory.*

It is also mentioned in the book of Psalm 80:1 and Psalm 99:1 - That God sits enthroned above the cherubim. Ezekiel also describes this very picture in the next scripture.

Ezekiel 1:22-23 (AMPC) - *Over the head of the [combined] living creatures was the likeness of a firmament, looking like the terrible and awesome [dazzling of shining] crystal or ice stretched across the expanse of the sky over their heads. And under the firmament their wings stretched out straight, one toward another... Verse 25 – And there was a voice above the firmament that was over their heads, when they stood, they let down their wings. And above the firmament that was over their heads was a likeness of a throne in appearance like a sapphire stone, and seated above the likeness of a throne was a likeness with appearance of a Man...*

Later we read it is the Lord God's voice speaking a message to Ezekiel.

The dictionary word for "firmament" mentioned means, the heavens or the sky! Especially when regarded as a tangible thing, the Hebrew word Raki'a for firmament simply means "expansion". In Genesis 1:6 - *God said let there be firmament.* In the next verse, *And God made the firmament,* and in the next verse again it states, *And God called the firmament Heavens.* So in the portion of Ezekiel, as Ezekiel mentions in his vision, that over their heads of the cherubim was the expanse of the heavens (the firmament), which is the bottom of the divine throne of God. In the other Bible scriptures, I mentioned that God sits enthroned above the Cherubim.

What an absolutely majestic, awesome and powerful mind blowing picture this displays for us. We can begin to see the magnificence and magnitude of the brilliance of the unseen realm and the existence of such glorious beings, and the operations and positions that they hold. Cherubim are the guardians and protectors of God's Holy Domain from any sin and corruption.

(C) SERAPHIM

Another type of angel named in the Bible is the seraphim angel. The word Seraphim is only called out once. That takes place in the book of Isaiah. But this passage provides us with an extremely important description of these powerful, magnificent and glorious beings.

> Isaiah 6:1-4 (AMPC) – *In the year that King Uzziah died, [in a vision] I saw the Lord sitting upon a throne, high and lifted up, and the skirts of His train filled the [most holy part of the] temple. Above Him stood the seraphim; each had six wings: with two [each] covered his [own] face, and with two [each] covered his feet, and with*

two [each] flew. And one cried to another and said, Holy, holy, holy is the Lord of hosts; the whole earth is full of His glory! And the foundations of the thresholds shook at the voice of him who cried, and the house was filled with smoke.

Now, unlike the cherubim having four wings, the seraphim angels have six wings each. Isaiah also reveals to us in this next verse that Seraphim have hands, although we are not exactly sure how many, or where they are located! Isaiah 6:6 (AMPC) - *Then flew one of the seraphim [heavenly beings] to me, having a live coal in his hand, which he had taken from off the altar.*

Now Isaiah viewed all this in a vision, and even the noble prophet was immediately convicted when this happened concerning his sin and the sins of Israel.

Scripture shows us that Isaiah was impacted to such an extent that he felt ruined and undone during this process. It shows us this in Isaiah 6:5 (AMPC) - *Then said I, "Woe is me! For I am undone and ruined, because I am a man of unclean lips, and I dwell in the midst of people with unclean lips; for my eyes have seen the King, the Lord of hosts"!*

In this portion it would appear that these heavenly hosts served as agents of purification for Isaiah as he began his prophetic ministry. The word, "Seraphim" is derived from the Hebrew word seraph, which means "to burn" or "burning ones". Seraphim angels burn with such a passion for God, that it ignites the fiery love that emanates from them.

The seraphim absorb God's pure love while spending time in His presence, and being completely enveloped by the powerful light of love which is described in the book called Song of Solomon chapter 8:6 (AMPC) - *Set me like a seal upon your heart, like a seal upon your arm; for love is as strong as death, jealousy is as hard and cruel as Sheol (the place of the dead). Its flashes are flashes of fire, a most vehement flame [the very flame of the Lord]!*

The word vehement means passionate, fervent, violent, strong, forceful, intense, powerful, earnest, keen, enthusiastic, zealous, ardent, heated, impassioned.

So, these angelic beings called seraphim are soaking up the incomprehensible light of God's Shekinah glory that defies the imagination. The life, love and light that flow from His very being has no metaphor or words in earthly language that can describe the supremely awesome sight that emanates from the very throne of God, with sparks of lightning and fire of vehement love 24 hours a day. They are forever in His presence above His throne and their primary duty is to constantly glorify and praise God.

Their eternal song is, *"Holy, Holy, Holy is the Lord of hosts; the whole earth is full of His glory"*. In Hebrew, to use the same word three times to describe something means the person/object is utterly like the word. So calling God Holy three times means God is utterly and perfectly Holy. Their resounding praise reverberates with such an awesome sound that it shakes the foundation of the heavenly temple.

So, as we gather together verses from the Bible we can start to build a picture of how things are in heaven. We can at least begin to perceive and calculate the height, width, the amplitude of such beings, and their strength and energy. The celestial skies being filled with perfect worship. Adoration being in the atmosphere constantly as the myriads of angels sing continually in their celestial languages of heaven in heaven, with sounds of worship in and around the very throne of Almighty God. At the sheer magnificence and brilliance of God's Shekinah[1], it streams forth from His presence for millions and millions of earth's miles, brighter than a billion sun stars, translucent and supremely awesome. Angels bidding at His every command; billions of commands, simultaneous commands coming forth from His very being. His omnipotence is more dazzling than we can even begin to describe and the weight of His Kabod[2] presence and glory is so overpowering you become floored and melt into nothingness at the Holiness and amplitude of Who He Is!

It tells us in Exodus 34, that after Moses went and met with the Lord, the skin of his face shone, so much so that the people feared to come near him until he covered it with a veil. In Matthew 17, it talks about Jesus taking Peter and James with Him up the

[1] Shekinah meaning "God's manifested glory" or "God's presence".

[2] Kabod meaning "glory", "respect", "honor", and "majesty".

mountain for a prayer meeting. Moses and Elijah showed up meeting them there and thus bringing heaven to earth, and how the appearance of Jesus underwent a change. His face shone as clear and bright like the sun and His clothing became as white as light. It also mentions that as they were gathered in Matthew 17:5-6 (AMPC) — *While he was still speaking, behold a shining cloud [composed of light] overshadowed them and a voice from the cloud said, "This is My Son, My Beloved, with Whom I am [and have always been] delighted. Listen to Him." When the disciples heard it, they fell on their faces and were seized with alarm and struck with fear.*

As mentioned earlier regarding the angel in Matthew 28, there was a great earthquake when an angel of the Lord descended from heaven. His appearance was like lightning and his garments as white as snow. Again the guards were frightened, agitated and fell like dead men.

Luke 2, this verse was also previously mentioned. But, this time it is to focus on the fact that the heavenly messenger angel stood by them, and the glory of the Lord flashed and shone all about them. They were also terribly frightened at such a glorious manifestation from another dimension, bringing it from the invisible realm into the visible.

These verses are just some of the experiences that real people, including Jesus, encountered while they were living life here on earth. Angelic beings come fresh from the throne room and the very presence of the Almighty God, and so the light of God's Shekinah glory is manifest on earth as it is in Heaven through their appearances.

(D) LIVING CREATURES

In the book of Revelation, the apostle John saw the living creatures as part of his heavenly vision. (An angel delivered the vision to John, His beloved disciple). So here we have an account of an angel publishing the vision for John and now we have another type of heavenly being mentioned in the Bible. It is the unveiling of divine mysteries.

Revelation 1:1 (MSG) - *A revealing of Jesus, the Messiah. God gave it to make plain to his servants what is about to happen. He published and delivered it by Angel to his servant John. And John told everything he saw: God's Word— the witness of Jesus Christ!*

It gives an account and describes the living creatures in Revelation 4:6-9 (AMPC) - *And in front of the throne there was also what looked like a transparent glassy sea, as if of crystal. And around the throne, in the center at each side of the throne, were four living creatures (beings) who were full of eyes in front and behind [with intelligence as to what is before and at the rear of them]. The first living creature (being) was like a lion, the second living creature like an ox, the third living creature had the face of a man, and the fourth living creature [was] like a flying eagle. And the four living creatures, individually having six wings, were full of eyes all over and within [underneath their wings]; and day and night they never stop saying, Holy, holy, holy is the Lord God Almighty*

(Omnipotent), Who was and Who is and Who is to come. And whenever the living creatures offer glory and honor and thanksgiving to Him Who sits on the throne, Who lives forever and ever (through the eternities of the eternities)...

John observed in his vision these four awesome living creatures, surrounding God's magnificent throne. The first living creature was like a lion, the second living creature like an ox, the third living creature had a face like a man, and the fourth living creature like a flying eagle. As like the cherubim, the faces are to remind the saints throughout all eternity of the earthly ministry performed by Lord Jesus.

Here is where the four living creatures differ from the cherubim. It tells us that each living creature around the throne has six wings, compared to the cherubim that possess four wings. Also, the living creatures have one face on the four separate beings whereas cherubim have four different faces on one individual being.

One purpose of the four living creatures is to declare the holiness of God and lead in worship and adoration of God. The worship from the living creatures is constant; without ceasing day and night, they proclaim... "Holy, Holy, Holy is the Lord God Almighty, Who was, Who is, and Who is to come!"

Another amazing fact it tells us is the living creatures are full of eyes in front and behind [with intelligence as to what is before and at the rear of them]. Also, we read that their six wings were full of eyes, all over and even underneath their wings. What a breathtaking and awesome sight to behold as they envelop and engage with the very throne of Almighty God.

It tells us when the living creatures offer glory and honor and thanksgiving to Him Who sits on the throne, others fall prostrate before His throne. Revelation 4:9-11 (AMPC) - *And whenever the living creatures offer glory and honor and thanksgiving to Him Who sits on the throne, Who lives forever and ever (through the eternities of the eternities), The twenty-four elders (the members of the heavenly Sanhedrin) fall prostrate before Him Who is sitting on the throne, and they worship Him Who lives forever and ever; and they throw down their crowns before the throne, crying out, "Worthy are You, our Lord and God, to receive the glory and the honor and dominion, for You created all things; by Your will they were [brought into being] and were created."*

These magnificent and breathtaking creatures are also revealed in other passages of the book of Revelation. Here are a few:

Revelation 5:8 (AMPC) - *And when He had taken the scroll, the four living creatures and the twenty-four elders of the heavenly Sanhedrin prostrated themselves before the Lamb...*

Revelation 6:1-7 (AMPC) - *Then I saw as the Lamb broke open one of the seven seals, and as if in a voice of thunder I heard one of the four living creatures call out, "Come!" And I looked, and saw there a white horse whose rider carried a bow. And a crown was given him,*

*and he rode forth conquering and to conquer. And when
He broke the second seal, I heard the second living
creature call out, "Come!" And another horse came out,
flaming red. And its rider was empowered to take the
peace from the earth, so that men slaughtered one another;
and he was given a huge sword. When He broke open the
third seal, I heard the third living creature call out,
"Come and look!" And I saw, and behold, a black
horse, and in his hand the rider had a pair of scales (a
balance). And I heard what seemed to be a voice from the
midst of the four living creatures, saying, "A quart of
wheat for a denarius [a whole day's wages], and three
quarts of barley for a denarius; but do not harm the oil
and the wine!" When the Lamb broke open the fourth
seal, I heard the fourth living creature call out, "Come!"*

So they are also involved with God's justice, for
when He opens the first four seals to send out the
four horsemen to destroy, the living creatures use
their powerful voices, like thunder, and command,
"Come". The horsemen respond to the summons of
the four powerful creatures, indicating the power the
creatures possess. That power is seen again
in Revelation 15 when one of the four unleashes the
last seven plagues of God's wrath on mankind.
Revelation 15:7 (AMPC) - *And one of the four living
creatures [then] gave the seven angels seven golden bowls full of
the wrath and indignation of God, Who lives forever and ever
(in the eternities of the eternities).*

Here are scriptures that should help us relate and understand a little more regarding the significance of the four faces of the cherubim and the living creatures and their positions. In the Bible, in the book of Numbers chapter 2, it tells us when Israel was camping in the wilderness, there was God's protection plan for the tabernacle (tent of meeting) containing the Shekinah glory of God's presence which was in their midst.

Scripture informs us that the earthly patterns given by God are often a shadow of a greater heavenly reality. Colossians 2:17 (AMPC) - *Such [things] are only the shadow of things that are to come, and they have only a symbolic value. But the reality (the substance, the solid fact of what is foreshadowed, the body of it) belongs to Christ.*

So it is not a great surprise when we find similarities between Israel's encampment in the wilderness around the tabernacle of meeting and the heavenly realm surrounding God's throne. Given the level of detail, which attends God's instructions concerning the encampment, it would be unusual if there were no symbolism to be found in it.

Numbers 2:1-3 (AMPC) - *The Lord said to Moses and Aaron, "The Israelites shall encamp, each by his own [tribal] standard or banner with the ensign of his father's house, opposite the Tent of Meeting and facing it on every side."*

The camp was to be set up as follows:

The Tabernacle of Meeting was in the center.

East - The camp of Judah, consisting of the tribes of Judah (74,800), Issachar (84,400), and Zebulun (57,400), a total of 186,400 men.

South - The camp of Reuben, consisting of the tribes of Reuben (46,500), Simeon (59,300), and Gad (45,650), a total of 151,450 men.

West - The camp of Ephraim, consisting of the tribes of Ephraim (40,500), Manasseh (32,200), and Benjamin (35,400), a total of 108,100 men.

North - The camp of Dan, consisting of the tribes of Dan (62,700), Asher (41,500), and Naphtali (53,400), a total of 157,600 men.

Each group was to camp by his own standard, the standards provided a visual rallying symbol for each camp when stationary and on the move. Every division was composed of three tribes. It denotes the army united under one standard with the banner of the tribe at the head of each division.

Neither the Mosaic Law nor the Old Testament generally gives us any intimation as to the form or character of the standard. However, according to rabbinical tradition, the standard of Judah bore the figure of a lion, that of Reuben the likeness of a man or of a man's head, that of Ephraim the figure of an ox, and that of Dan the figure of an eagle; so that the four living creatures united in the cherubic forms described by Ezekiel were represented upon these four standards.

Now these camping positions (arranged according to compass directions) also dictated marching orders: that is who marched in the lead, who followed next and so on, down to who brought up the rear.

Numbers 2:17 (AMPC) - *Then the Tent of Meeting shall set out, with the camp of the Levites in the midst of the camps; as they encamp so shall they set forward, every man in his place, standard after standard.*

The Levites (priests), carrying and protecting the all-important tent shrine, were to be smack dab in the middle of the marching column. So the Tabernacle was always in the center surrounded by 12 tribes, day and night. Just like the throne of God surrounded and protected by the magnificent guardians of Heaven.

(E) GUARDIAN ANGELS

"For He will command His angels concerning you to guard you in all your ways," reads Psalm 91:11. The writer of this Psalm is recognizing God's ability to send down help to His creation through angelic means. The faithful are under the constant care and guidance of angels. Then in Psalm 91:11-12 (AMPC) - *For He will give His angels [especial] charge over you to accompany and defend and preserve you in all your ways [of obedience and service]. They shall bear you up on their hands, lest you dash your foot against a stone].*

The enemy uses this very same scripture in Luke 4 quoting it to Jesus saying, Luke 4:9-11 (AMPC) - *If you are the Son of God, cast yourself down from here. For it is written. He will give His angels charge over you to guard and watch over you closely and carefully, and on their hands they will bear you up, lest you strike your foot against a stone.*

So the enemy also knows that we have angels that guard us. That's why they are called guardian angels. They are sent to guard and protect us from harm. When we get to Heaven, we will discover that much of what we thought was chance, coincidence and providence was in fact, the action of our guardian angel functioning as our protector.

Given the words of Matthew 18:10 (AMPC) - ... *for I tell you that in Heaven their angels always are in the presence of and look upon the face of My Father Who is in Heaven.* Now the word (their) means – belonging to or associated with the people or things mentioned. It is showing us we each have our very own specific guardian.

The Message bible reads the same verse in Matthew this way... *that Jesus said we each have a heavenly angel who is before the throne of God.* Matthew 18:10 (MSG) - *Watch that you don't treat a single one of these childlike believers arrogantly. You realize, don't you that their personal angels are constantly in touch with the Father in Heaven?*

This is Jesus saying that God Himself is distinctly recognizing the existence of guardian angels assigned to individuals and God is caring for His people through angelic means. These angels always see the face of God and it is important to see here that angels are superior to man. However, they are not omnipotent; they do not know all things at all times.

God however does, and if our angels are always in communion with God at all times they know when we have a need, when we hurt and when we stray. They can be here for us in exactly the ways in which we need, channeling God's love at all times. We could ask for nothing better in our guardian angel or angels.

The writer of Hebrews said that angels are commissioned to aid and minister to believers here in this natural realm. Hebrews 1:14 (AMPC) – *"Are not the angels all ministering spirits (servants) sent out in the service [of God for the assistance] of those who are to inherit salvation?"*

This verse speaks of angels as servants being "ministering spirits". The focus of this passage is on the importance of mankind as Jesus Christ's heirs. Angels are shown to be our protectors, beings who minister to us in opposing the power of evil spirits, and in guiding us, both spiritually and physically. These angels are sent to those *"who will inherit salvation"* the faithful, those who have come to the Father through Christ Jesus.

It is important that we pray for this protection. As beings of the flesh, we have no power to combat spiritual entities in the natural, however it is entirely possible to break negativity in your life through faithful prayer. God will send angels to help you, which as we learned earlier, always have their face turned toward the omnipotence of God, and will instantly know your needs and come to your aid.

Since we know that bad things, at times, happen to

all of us, we don't know exactly in what way our angels are guarding us. But, that doesn't mean that they are not! I said earlier, when we finally reach heaven, we may find they safeguarded us from thousands of ills and troubles that we could have never imagined. Since God is all-knowing, we must assume that these angels keep us safe in exactly the ways we need most - no more, no less. Take comfort in knowing that God has assigned an angel to guard you in the best ways possible.

Psalm 34:6-7 (AMPC) - *This poor man cried, and the Lord heard him, and saved him out of all his troubles. The Angel of the Lord encamps around those who fear Him [who revere and worship Him with awe] and each of them He delivers.*

The dictionary meaning of the word, "encamp" is to settle in or establish a camp, especially a military one and the dictionary meaning for "around" is located or situated on every side.

So He places (encamps) with us a protecting angel to guide us and keep us safe. It is important to remember that all power flows down from God. The angels are His servants, that He sends down to care for us. When we pray, we should direct our supplications to the Father, to the one who created us and who knows us best. Send your prayers for angelic protection up to God, and He will ensure that you'll receive it.

As we can see in Psalm 34, God does send His angels to aid us, we may even each have our own protector assigned to watch over us from the moment we gain our faith. These angels are powerful, capable of defending us against spiritual attack, influencing us to be morally good, and even physically rescuing us from dangerous situations. All of these precedents are provided for us in scripture.

Remember our ultimate guardian is God, ruler of the angels. He is in all places at all times, and knows all things. He is our ever-present protector. It is through Him the angels receive their directives, helping us mortals throughout our lives, comforting, protecting, and keeping us through His love.

It tells us in this verse that angels hearken to the voice of God's (His) Word. Psalm 103:20-22 (AMPC) - *Bless (affectionately, gratefully praise) the Lord, you His angels, you mighty ones who do His commandments, hearkening to the voice of His word. Bless (affectionately, gratefully praise) the Lord, all you His hosts, you His ministers who do His pleasure. Bless the Lord, all His works in all places of His dominion; bless (affectionately, gratefully praise) the Lord, O my soul!*

Notice that the verse says that angels are "hearkening to the voice of His word". To clarify greater the word hearken means to listen, so the angels are listening for the promises of God to be released, Now who gives voice to God's Word? We do! Each time we speak God's Word, we give voice to His Word. And when angels hear His Word given voice, they respond!

The Bible says that at the end of Daniel's three weeks of fasting and praying for an answer from God, the angel Gabriel appeared to Daniel and said to him, *"I have come because of your words"*. (Daniel 10:12)

This is so exciting, it is showing us that we can do this, that this is an opportunity to utilize if we just use our voice and put sound to "The Word of God". Then angels go to work. So when angels hear you saying, *"Thank You, Father, that no evil shall befall me nor shall any plague come near my dwelling,"* (Psalm 91:10), they will come to your aid because you are giving voice to God's Word. Even if you cannot quote the verse perfectly, they can still come to your rescue.

Another example you can say/declare/pray, "Thank you, Father you said in Your Word that no weapon formed against me will prosper". (Isaiah 54:17). Know this, that the sound of your voice is powerful and it is activating and releasing angels and putting them to work on your behalf. As you declare God's Word, angels are being dispatched to fulfill His Word!

However, even if you know God's Word by heart but refuse to proclaim it, the power of His Word cannot be released. The Bible does not say that angels heed His Word. No, it says that *"His angels, who excel in strength, who do His word, heeding the voice of His word"*. So let's give voice to God's Word and see His angels respond. His angels are activated for your benefit when you speak His Word!

LEAH LEAMAN

11

ANGELS: AT WORK/IN ACTION

This is where we see God sending angels to help minister to people. When Elijah felt like he was ready to give up on life, the Lord sent an angel to minister to him. 1 Kings 19:5-7 (AMPC) - *As he lay asleep under the broom or juniper tree, behold, an angel touched him and said to him, "Arise and eat." He looked, and behold there was a cake baked on the coals, and a bottle of water at his head. And he ate and drank and lay down again. The angel of the Lord came the second time and touched him and said, "Arise and eat, for the journey is too great for you."*

The angel came, touched and ministered to Elijah in his time of great need. Just when it seemed he was down to nothing, God sent a Heavenly messenger to minister to him.

Likewise, in Daniel 6:19 we discover a powerful angel was dispatched to shut the mouths of the hungry lions while Daniel was in their den. Daniel 6:22 (AMPC) - *My God has sent His angel and has shut the lions mouths so that they have not hurt me, because I was found innocent and blameless before Him; and also before you, O king. I have done no harm or wrong.*

Again angels are put into action in the book of Acts. There are two miraculous escapes from prison recorded in this book here is the first in Acts 5:18-20 (AMPC) - *They seized and arrested the apostles (special messengers) and put them in jail. But during the night an angel of the Lord opened the prison doors and, leading them out said, "Go, take your stand in the temple courts and declare to the people the whole doctrine concerning this Life" (the eternal life which Christ revealed).*

The second is in this next portion of scripture. It shows us a time when King Herod wanted to oppress and torment some who belonged to the church, so he arrested Peter. Now it says in verse 4 that Peter was delivered to four squads of soldiers, of four each, to guard him… That's a lot of soldiers for one man! Then an angel of the Lord intervened. The following happens:

> Acts 12:6-11 (AMPC) - *The very night before Herod was about to bring him forth, Peter was sleeping between two soldiers, fastened with two chains, and sentries before the door were guarding the prison. And suddenly an angel of the Lord appeared [standing beside him], and a light shone in the place where he was. And the angel gently smote Peter on the side and awakened him, saying, "Get up quickly!" And the chains fell off his hands. And the angel said to him, "Tighten your belt and bind on your sandals." And he did so. And he said to him, "Wrap*

your outer garment around you and follow me." And [Peter] went out [along] following him, and he was not conscious that what was apparently being done by the angel was real, but thought he was seeing a vision. When they had passed through the first guard and the second, they came to the Iron Gate, which leads into the city. Of, its own accord [the gate] swung open, and they went out and passed on through one street; and at once the angel left him. Then Peter came to himself and said, "Now I really know and am sure that the Lord has sent His angel and delivered me from the hand of Herod and from all that the Jewish people were expecting [to do to me]."

Although the last portion in Acts 12 is quite lengthy, I wanted us to see the full picture and measure of all the miraculous, supernatural things that happened in this portion of scripture!

To review, firstly an angel of the Lord appeared suddenly inside a locked prison cell beside Peter, where he was sleeping between two bodyguards, who are guarding him intently. Their life was on the line. So, they would have been 100% determined that nothing would happen to Peter under their watch.

The light shone brightly from this heavenly being. Can you imagine the illumination that was taking place? Then the angel touched Peter on his side to awaken him from his sleep, and gave him instruction to get up, quickly. Remember, Peter, was also bound by two chains. Then the chains supernaturally fell off and he got up and was able to get dressed. In the meantime the guards seemed oblivious to what was going on in their midst all this time.

Peter also didn't seem to realize what was actually happening. Instead, he thought he was having a vision of some sort! Next the angel said to Peter "Follow me". Then they walked straight out through the prison door, passing two other guards (sentries) that were stationed there who did not notice either. As Peter recalls, they just passed by them!

Then they went out through an iron gate that led to the city streets, which supernaturally swung open of its own accord and after they had passed through one street the angel suddenly left him. The experience had such a profound effect on Peter that he knew without a shadow of a doubt the Lord had sent His angel to deliver him from Herod.

Reading of these breathtaking experiences makes us realize these spiritual encounters do happen. The miraculous power of God unfolding and working on behalf of His people is outrageously amazing and supernaturally fascinating, defying all odds!

In the next part of the encounter, it goes on to say, that he continued onto Mary's house where there were a large number of people praying for him. When he knocked at the gate, Rhoda went to answer the knock and heard Peter's voice. You can read a portion of the scripture here:

Acts 12:13-15 (NIV) - *Peter knocked at the outer entrance, and a servant named Rhoda came to answer the door. When she recognized Peter's voice, she was so overjoyed she ran back without opening it and exclaimed, "Peter is at the door!" "You're out of your mind," they told her. When she kept insisting that it was so, they said, "It must be his angel".*

Isn't it strange, that it was easier for those praying, to believe it was Peter's angel at the gate rather than the fact that their prayers were answered and it was actually the man himself? They also seemed to be aware and confident in knowing that we have angels and also that they look and sound like us, very interesting, using the phrase (It must be his angel) in this case, like it's no unusual thing to believe or accept.

12

ANGELS: WE ARE
LOWER THAN

To help show us the ranking of how we are placed, it says in Hebrews that He made us (mankind) a little lower than the angels. It also tells us in this portion that Jesus was also made a little lower than the angels for a little while, when He was born here on earth and lived as a man for 33 years. Then, after His death by crucifixion and resurrection three days later, He was crowned with glory and honor in Heaven, because He suffered death, so that by the grace of God He tasted death for everyone. Read the scripture:

> Hebrews 2:6-10 (NIV) - *But there is a place where someone has testified: "What is mankind that you are mindful of them, a son of man that you care for him? You made them a little lower than the angels; you crowned them with glory and honor and put everything under their feet." In putting everything under them, God left nothing that is not subject to them. Yet at present we*

do not see everything subject to them. But we do see Jesus, who was made lower than the angels for a little while, now crowned with glory and honor because he suffered death, so that by the grace of God he might taste death for everyone. In bringing many sons and daughters to glory, it was fitting that God, for whom and through whom everything exists, should make the pioneer of their salvation perfect through what he suffered.

The angels are somewhat baffled that God continues to extend grace to fallen humanity. The angels are curious about this, or as Peter put it, they desire to understand.

1 Peter 1:12 (MEV) - *It was revealed to them that they were not serving themselves but you, concerning the things which are now reported to you by those who have preached the gospel to you through the Holy Spirit, who was sent from heaven—things into which the angels desire to look.*

13

ANGELS: PERSONALITIES

It is so exciting to dive into the Bible and open up scriptures to discover and enlighten our minds into what we so often overlook and gloss over. But as we delve into some of these details, we develop a greater clarity and revelation of certain things that cause understanding to then take place. Some might be surprised to discover that angels have varying personalities.

Firstly we need to define what having a personality means. It includes three necessary features: intelligence, emotion and will. So, as we open up the Word of God it reveals that angels have personality. Even the previous verse shows us they have a curious nature, as they desire to look into things and gain greater understanding. So, within their personality they display desire. Another emotion they display is joy, as we read in Luke 15:10 (NKJV) – *"Likewise, I say to you, there is joy in the presence of the angels of God over one sinner who repents."*

Luke 2:13-14 (NKJV) - *And suddenly there was with the angel a multitude of the heavenly host praising God and saying: "Glory to God in the highest, And on earth peace, goodwill toward men!"*

Hebrews 12:22 (NIV) - *But you have come to Mount Zion, to the city of the living God, the heavenly Jerusalem. You have come to thousands upon thousands of angels in joyful assembly.*

Angels carry emotions, the excitement of sharing good news and delivering heavenly messages. We also conclude that angels have a will, which is revealed in the actions of the rebellion against God in heaven. They chose to do this! We see within himself, Satan said five times "I will"!

Isaiah 14:12-15 (TLB) - *How you are fallen from heaven, O Lucifer, son of the morning! How you are cut down to the ground—mighty though you were against the nations of the world. For you said to yourself, "I will ascend to heaven and rule the angels. I will take the highest throne. I will preside on the Mount of Assembly far away in the north. I will climb to the highest heavens and be like the Most High." But instead, you will be brought down to the pit of hell, down to its lowest depths.*

Now onto the next aspect, which is intelligence. Scripture acknowledges their knowledge. Gabriel shows us in the book of Daniel and making a statement to Daniel that he had come to give him skill and wisdom and understanding. Daniel 9:21-22 (AMPC) - *Yes, while I was speaking in prayer, the man Gabriel, whom I had seen in the former vision, being caused to fly swiftly, came near to me and touched me about the time of the evening sacrifice. He instructed me and made me understand; he talked with me and said, "O Daniel, I am now come forth to give you skill and wisdom and understanding."*

Remember what was written in the chapter quoted earlier from the book of Hebrews? It says we are ranked a little lower than the angels. Therefore their intelligence is beyond that of humans. In addition, their intelligence has not been corrupted by sin, as is the case with humanity.

Again, we see this when Michael the angel was enlightening Daniel through delivering an important message, to help make Daniel understand and to prepare him for what to expect in the days to come for his people. Daniel in 10:13-14 (AMPC) - *But the prince of the kingdom of Persia withstood me for twenty-one days. Then Michael, one of the chief [of the celestial] princes, came to help me, for I remained there with the kings of Persia. Now I have come to make you understand what is to befall your people in the latter days, for the vision is for [many] days yet to come.*

You can see from scripture that angels indeed do have personality, as well as many other characteristics that set them apart from humanity. This enables them to be able to serve God's plan, as they do the tasks that are set before them both in heaven and on earth.

LEAH LEAMAN

14

ANGELS: THEIR ROLES

Here is just a quick recap from the Word of God of some of the roles that angels are involved in. However, remember angels are a highly organized hierarchy, which Christ sovereignly rules, and reigns. There is no way to be able to number all the diverse actions and activities of angels. A few are listed below with a scripture reference to corroborate.

They worship and praise Almighty God. This is the main activity portrayed in Heaven. Revelation 5:11-12; Psalm 103:20-22; Isaiah 6:1-3; Hebrews 1:6.

They protect. Psalm 91:11; Daniel 6:22; Genesis 19:10; Psalm 34:7; Matthew 2:13

They deliver. Psalm 34:7; Acts 5:19; Acts 12:7-10

They encourage. Acts 27:23-25; Acts 5:19

They inform and instruct. Daniel 9:21-22; Genesis 19:15; Acts 1:10-11; 1 Kings 19:5-8; 1 Chronicles 21:18; Joshua 5:15

They strengthen. Daniel 10:18-19; Matthew 4:11; Luke 22:43

They comfort. Acts 27:23-24; Matthew 18:10; Psalm 91:11-12; Zachariah 1:13

They guide. Acts 8:26; Acts 10:3-6; Numbers 20:16; 1 Chronicles 21:18

They are messengers. Psalm 104:4; Luke 2:10-12; Hebrews 2:2; Luke 1:30-33; Luke 1:36; Luke 1:19

They answer prayer. Acts 12:5-17

They minister to children of God. Hebrews 1:14; 1 Kings 19:5-8

They destroy. 2 Samuel 24:16; Psalm 78:49; 1 Chronicles 21:15

They wrestle. Genesis 32:25

They bring healing. John 5:4

We can see that angels are intended for various activities both in heaven and here on earth. They always have been since the beginning of time. The more we learn to partner with them and see how they operate, the more we can put them to work and learn how to partner with them in our everyday lives and advance the Kingdom of God! It is our job to make and keep them busy…isn't that an awesome thought! The Word of God calls them "ministering spirits" sent out to aid us. But, they are waiting for us to commission them by declaring God's Word and putting them to action.

When we go into a restaurant, there is either a man

(waiter) or woman (waitress) waiting on you to take your order. They are not going to tell you what you are going to order. They are waiting on you to tell them what to bring from the menu selection given. That is the way it is with angels. They are around us waiting to be activated by us praying to God, and speaking out the Word of God to Our Heavenly Father. That will then commission them to be released on our behalf.

It tells us in John 14:13 (AMPC) - *And I will do [I Myself will grant] whatever you ask in My Name [as presenting all that I AM], so that the Father may be glorified and extolled in (through) the Son.*

Let's say we want to secure protection from harm over our self or on behalf of someone else. Here is an example of how you might pray:

Thank you, Lord, for Your many promises of protection. I pray that You will put a hedge of safety and protection around (name) on every side and keep (name) away from harm. Protect (name) from any hidden dangers and let no weapon formed against (name) to prosper. Help (name) to walk in obedience to Your will so that (name) never comes out from under the umbrella of that protection. Keep (name) safe in all (name) does and wherever (name) goes. In Jesus' name, I pray.

Now within that prayer of declaration was at least seven Bible verses from The Word of God. They are listed next:

Job 1:10 (AMPC) - *Have You not put a hedge about him and his house and all that he has, on every side? You have conferred prosperity and happiness upon him in the work of his hands, and his possessions have increased in the land.*

Psalm 91:9-11 (AMPC) (GNT) - *You have made the Lord your defender, the Most High your protector, and so no disaster will strike you, no violence will come near your home. God will put his angels in charge of you to protect you wherever you go.*

Isaiah 54:17 (AMP) - *"No weapon that is formed against you will succeed; And every tongue that rises against you in judgment you will condemn. This [peace, righteousness, security, and triumph over opposition] is the heritage of the servants of the Lord, And this is their vindication from Me," says the Lord.*

Psalm 91:1 (AMPC) - *He who dwells in the shelter of the Most High, will remain secure and rest in the shadow of the Almighty [whose power no enemy can withstand].*

John 14:13 (AMPC) - *And I will do [I Myself will grant] whatever you ask in My Name [as presenting all that I Am], so that the Father may be glorified and extolled in (through) the Son.*

Hebrews 13:5 (GNT) - *Keep your lives free from the love of money, and be satisfied with what you have. For God has said, "I will never leave you; I will never abandon you."*

Philippians 4:6 (AMP) - *Do not be anxious or worried about anything, but in everything [every circumstance and situation] by prayer and petition with thanksgiving, continue to make your [specific] requests known to God.*

So that gives us an example of how to pray/declare the Word of God to release angels on our behalf. As we continue to pray daily (ask) and put our requests to God, the Bible tells us that He hears our requests, and angels serve Him and obey His Word. The angels are being activated and put to work.

Psalm 103:20 (AMP) - *Bless the LORD, you His angels, You mighty ones who do His commandments, obeying the voice of His word. Bless the LORD, all you His hosts, You who serve Him and do His will.*

15

THE ANGEL OF THE LORD

This Angel is specifically described as "The Angel", not 'an angel', or 'the angels'. It is also always singular usage and never plural, and also usually the first letter is always uppercase/capitalized in the Bible, and so forth, to identify it being a title or a name.

Always being referred to in the Bible as, "The Angel of the Lord" or, "The Angel of God" or, "The Angel of His Presence" and is readily identified with the Lord God. The "Angel of the Lord" is a distinct person in Himself from God the Father. The "Angel of the Lord" does not appear again after Jesus came in human form. He seemed to be, however, "The visible Lord God of the Old Testament, as Jesus Christ is of the New Testament. This is why His deity is clearly portrayed in the Old Testament with little glimpses from Genesis through to Malachi.

In some instances, it is made clear that the reference is to a theophany. This comes from two Greek words, (theo) meaning "God," and (phaino) which means "appear"—(which means a visible manifestation to humankind of God) acting on His Own behalf rather than using a separate entity.

The following are examples of use of the term "Angel of the Lord":

In Genesis 16:7-14 (AMPC) verse seven starts with the words - *But the Angel of the Lord found her… So the Angel of the Lord appears to Hagar, the Angel of the Lord speaks as God.* And in verse 13 (NIV) of that passage it says – *She gave this name to the LORD who spoke to her: "You are the God who sees me," for she said, "I have now seen the One who sees me."*

Next in Genesis 22:11-17 (AMPC) verse 11 starts with the words - *But the Angel of the Lord called to him from Heaven and said…* So the Angel of the Lord called from Heaven to stop Abraham from giving his son as a sacrifice in an act of obedience. It mentions in verse 15 (NLT) of that passage - *"This is what the LORD says: Because you have obeyed me and have not withheld even your son, your only son, I swear by my own name that…* So the Lord was referring to Himself here and swearing by His own name being God in the first person.

And again in Exodus, the Angel of the Lord this time appeared to Moses, it reads… Exodus 3:2-6 (AMPC) - *The Angel of the Lord appeared to him in a flame of fire out of the midst of a bush; and he looked, and behold, the bush burned with fire, yet was not consumed. And Moses said, "I will now turn aside and see this great sight, why the bush is not burned." And when the Lord saw that he turned aside to see, God called to him out of the midst of the bush and said, "Moses, Moses!" And he said, "Here am I." God said,*

"Do not come near; put your shoes off your feet, for the place on which you stand is holy ground." Also He said, "I am the God of your father, the God of Abraham, the God of Isaac, and the God of Jacob." And Moses hid his face, for he was afraid to look at God.

Again, the Angel of the Lord is identified as none other than, "the Lord" Himself. The God of his father and so forth, and the bush was not consumed! That's supernatural all in itself.

In the book of Numbers is another account where the Angel of the Lord is mentioned. Numbers 22:22-35 (AMPC) tells us when the Angel of the Lord stood in the way of Balaam's donkey with His sword drawn in His hand. Here is the abbreviated story:

Balaam set off on a journey to do some sorcery work for Balak, the king of ancient Moab, in exchange for a large sum of money. Even though God had sent a message in a dream not to do the work, which involved spiritually cursing the Israelite people whom God had blessed, Balaam let greed take over in his soul and chose to take on the Moabite assignment despite God's warning. God was angry that Balaam was motivated by greed rather than faithfulness.

As Balaam was riding on his donkey on the way to do the work, God himself showed up in angelic form as the Angel of the Lord. Numbers 22:23 (AMPC) describes what happened next - *And the donkey saw the Angel of the Lord standing in the way and His sword drawn in His hand, and the donkey turned aside out of the way and went into the field. And Balaam struck the donkey to turn her into the way.*

Balaam went on to beat his donkey twice more as the donkey continued to move out of the Angel of the Lord's way. Each time the donkey moved abruptly, Balaam got upset by the sudden movement and decided to punish his animal. The donkey could see the Angel of the Lord, but Balaam couldn't. Ironically, even though Balaam was a famous sorcerer who was known for his clairvoyant abilities, he couldn't see God appearing as an Angel – but one of God's creatures could. Then, miraculously, God made it possible for the donkey to speak to Balaam in an audible voice to get his attention.

> Numbers 22:28 (AMPC) - *Then the LORD opened the donkey's mouth, and it said to Balaam, "What have I done to you to make you strike me these three times?"*

Balaam replied that the donkey has made him feel foolish, and then threatens in Numbers 22:29 (AMPC) - *"I wish there were a sword in my hand, for now I would kill you"!*

The donkey spoke again, reminding Balaam of its faithful service to him every day for a long time, and asking if it had ever upset Balaam before. Balaam admitted the donkey had not. God opens Balaam's eyes in verse 31 - *"Then the LORD opened Balaam's eyes, and he saw the Angel of the Lord standing in the way with His sword drawn in His hand".*

Balaam then fell down on the ground. But his

demonstration of reverence was probably motivated more by fear than by respect for God, since he was still determined to take the job that King Balak had offered to pay him for, but which God had warned him against! God, in angelic form, then confronted Balaam about how he had abused his donkey through the severe beatings. Verses 32 and 33 describe what God said: *The angel of the Lord said to him, "Why have you struck your donkey these three times? See, I came out to stand against and resist you, for your behavior is willfully obstinate and contrary before Me. And the ass saw Me and turned from Me three times. If she had not turned from Me, surely I would have slain you and saved her alive".*

God's declaration that he would definitely have killed Balaam if not for the donkey turning away from his sword must have been shocking and sobering news for Balaam. Not only did God see how he had mistreated an animal, but also God took that mistreatment quite seriously. Balaam realized that it was actually because of the donkey's attempts to protect him that his life was spared. The kindhearted creature he had beaten was only trying to help him and indeed, ended up saving his life.

Balaam replied, *"I have sinned"* (verse 34) and then agreed to say only what God instructed him to say during the meeting to which he was traveling... So the encounter changed the outcome.

So, interesting that the donkey could see the Angel of the Lord and Balaam could not until the Lord opened Balaam's eyes in Verse 31. As soon as his eyes were enlightened and he saw the Angel of the Lord already with His sword drawn, then Balaam bowed his head and fell on his face! That definitely got his attention!

Here are a few more places that the Angel of the Lord are mentioned. I will let you look up the content for yourselves for further clarification!

Judges chapter 2:1-4
The Angel of the Lord appears to Israel.

Judges 6:11-23
The Angel of the Lord appears to Gideon.

Judges 13:3-22
The Angel of the Lord appears to Manoah and his wife.

Zachariah 3
The Angel of the Lord defends Joshua.

Psalm 34:7
The Angel of the Lord encamps around those who fear Him.

Psalm 35:5
David mentions the Angel of the Lord in his distress.

16

ANGEL OF GOD

As I said earlier, the term "Angel of God" occurs in the Old Testament of the Bible and the usage of the name for God here is (Elohim). It is a Hebrew word that denotes "God" and it is one of the most common names for God in the Old Testament, starting in the very first verse: Genesis 1:1 - *"In the beginning* [Elohim] *created the heavens and the earth"*. The basic meaning behind the name Elohim is one of strength, or power, or effect. Elohim is the infinite, all-powerful God who shows by His works that He is the Creator, Sustainer, and Supreme Judge of the world.

Genesis 31:11 – *The Angel of God calls out to Jacob in a dream and tells Jacob "I am the God of Bethel".*

Exodus 14:19 – *The Angel of God leads the camp of Israel and also went behind them.*

Judges 13:9 – *God listened to the voice of Manoah. So*

the Angel of God came again and approached the
wife of Manoah.

Genesis 32:24-29 – *...then Jacob asked Him, "Tell*
me, I pray you, what [in contrast] is Your name?" But
He said, "Why is it that you ask My name?" And the
Angel of God declared a blessing on Jacob there, and
Jacob called the name of the place Peniel [the face of
God], saying, "For I have seen the God face to face..."

17

GOD SENDING AN ANGEL

Examples from scripture:

Exodus 23:20-21 (AMPC) – *"Behold, I send an Angel before you to keep you and guard you on the way and to bring you to the place I have prepared. Give heed to Him, listen to and obey His voice; be not rebellious before Him or provoke Him for He will not pardon your transgressions; for My Name is in Him".*

Exodus 33:2 (AMPC) - *The Lord said to Moses, "I will send an Angel before you, and I will drive out the Canaanite, Amorite, Hittite, Perizzite, the Hivite, and the Jebusite."*

Numbers 20:16 (AMPC) - *But when we cried to the Lord, He heard us and sent an angel and brought us forth out of Egypt...*

1 Chronicles 21:15-16 (AMPC) - *God sent an angel to Jerusalem to destroy it, and as he was destroying, the Lord beheld, and He regretted and relented of the evil and said to the destroying angel, "It is enough; now stay your hand." And the angel of the Lord stood by the threshing floor of Ornan the Jebusite. David lifted up his eyes and saw the angel of the Lord standing between earth and the heavens, having a drawn sword in his hand stretched out over Jerusalem...*

2 Chronicles 32:21 (AMPC) - *And the Lord sent an angel, who cut off all the mighty warriors and commanders and officers in the camp of the king of Assyria...*

18

ANGELS: OTHER REFERENCES

Matthew 13:41 (AMPC) - *The Son of Man will send forth His angels, and they will gather out of His kingdom all causes of offense and all who do iniquity and act wickedly...*

John 1:51 (AMPC) - *Then He said to him, "I assure you, most solemnly I tell you all, you shall see heaven opened, and the angels of God ascending and descending upon the Son of Man!"*

Genesis 28:12 (AMPC) - Jacob's dream - *And he dreamed that there was a ladder set up on the earth, and the top of it reached to heaven; and the angels of God were ascending and descending on it!*

There are so many scriptures that mention angels and their interaction with us whether in dreams or reality that it astounds me. As I search the Word for more on the subject, I find I could go on and on as more arise! We tend to gloss over so many of them in our day-to-day devotional time. The angel assignments can vary in so many ways, and there is such an extensive list of roles that angels fulfill: action towards believers; action towards Israel; action toward the unsaved; action towards Christ; activities in heaven toward the Godhead; and activities here on earth with us.

19

ANGELS: IN THE
BOOK OF REVELATION

The revelation proceeds from God to Jesus Christ through the angel to one servant in particular, named John (known as the beloved disciple of Jesus). John was the recipient of this vision and he addressed the long letter of "John" to the seven churches with which he was familiar. The book of Revelation is often known as the Apocalypse of the New Testament.

So in the last book of the Bible the "Book of Revelation", angels play a prominent role. There are countless times where angels are mentioned from preaching the everlasting gospel, to the binding of Satan into the pit. Angels are in the midst of the program of God at the end times. Consequently, angels have been an important part of God's dealings with humanity from Genesis through to Revelation.

Here are a few scriptures of their involvement in the book of Revelation and the roles they play:

In Revelation we find innumerable angels worshipping around the throne!

Revelation 5:11 (AMPC) - *Then I looked, and I heard the voice of many angels surrounding the throne and the living creatures and the elders; they numbered myriads of myriads and thousands of thousands.*

Four angels restrain the winds of judgment upon the earth!

Revelation 7:1 (AMPC) - *After this I saw four angels stationed at the four corners of the earth, firmly holding back the four winds of the earth so that no wind should blow on the earth or sea or upon any tree.*

Seven angels sound seven trumpets of Judgment!

Revelation 8:2-3 (AMPC) - *Then I saw the seven angels who stand before God, and to them were given seven trumpets. And another angel came and stood over the altar...*

Under the leadership of Michael the archangel, angels will be fighting in heaven!

Revelation 12:7-9 (AMPC) - *Then war broke out in heaven; Michael and his angels went forth to battle with the dragon, and the dragon and his angels fought. But they were defeated, and there was no room found for them in heaven any longer. And the huge dragon was cast*

*down and out—that age-old serpent, who is called the
Devil and Satan, he who is the seducer (deceiver) of all
humanity the world over; he was forced out and down to
the earth, and his angels were flung out along with him.*

Worldwide preaching of the Eternal Gospel by an angel!

Revelation 14:6 (AMPC) - *Then I saw another angel
flying in midair, with an eternal Gospel (good news) to
tell to the inhabitants of the earth, to every race and tribe
and language and people.*

An angel will announce the fall of Babylon!

Revelation 14:8-9 (AMPC) - *Then another angel, a
second, followed, declaring, fallen, fallen is Babylon the
great! She who made all nations drink of the
[maddening] wine of her passionate unchastity [idolatry].
Then another angel, a third, followed them saying...*

The wicked will be judged in the presence of angels!

Revelation 14:10 (AMPC) - *... and he shall be
tormented with fire and brimstone in the presence of the
holy angels and in the presence of the Lamb.*

The angels are to become harvesters at the end time. Both good and evil!

Revelation 14:17-19 (AMPC) - *Then another angel came out of the temple [sanctuary] in heaven, and he also carried a sharp scythe (sickle). And another angel came forth from the altar, [the angel] who has authority and power over fire, and he called with a loud cry to him who had the sharp scythe (sickle), Put forth your scythe and reap the fruitage of the vine of the earth, for its grapes are entirely ripe. So the angel swung his scythe on the earth and stripped the grapes and gathered the vintage from the vines of the earth and cast it into the huge winepress of God's indignation and wrath.*

Before Christ returns, angels will pour out seven bowls of judgment on the people of the earth!

Revelation 15:1 (AMPC) - *... there were seven angels bringing seven plagues (afflictions, calamities) which are the last, for with them God's wrath is (indignation) is completely expressed [reaches its climax and is ended].*

An angel reveals the great harlot to John!

Revelation 17:1 (AMPC) - *One of the seven angels who had the seven bowls then came and spoke with me, saying, "Come with me! I will show you the doom (sentence, judgment) of the great harlot (idolatress) who is seated on many waters".*

An angel calls for judgment of the people!

Revelation 19:17 (AMPC) - *Then I saw a single angel stationed in the suns light and with a mighty voice he shouted to all the birds that fly across the sky, "Come, gather yourselves together for the great supper of God..."*

After Christ returns, an angel will bind Satan in the pit for a thousand years!

Revelation 20:1-3 (AMPC) - *Then I saw an angel descending from heaven; he was holding the key of the Abyss (the bottomless pit) and a great chain was in his hand. And he gripped and overpowered the dragon, that old serpent [of primeval times], who is the devil and Satan, and [securely] bound him for a thousand years. Then he hurled him into the Abyss (the bottomless pit) and closed it and sealed it above him, so that he should no longer lead astray and deceive and seduce the nations until the thousand years were at an end. After that he must be liberated for a short time.*

20

KINGDOM AGE AND BEYOND

God's angels have a wonderful destiny, to spend eternity in the New Jerusalem, along with the elect saints of God.

Hebrews 12:22-24 (AMPC) - *But rather, you have come to Mount Zion, even to the city of the living God, the heavenly Jerusalem, and to countless multitudes of angels in festal gathering, and to the church (assembly) of the firstborn who are registered [as citizens] in heaven, and to the God Who is Judge of all, and to the spirits of the righteous (the redeemed in heaven) who have been made perfect, And to Jesus, the Mediator (Go between, Agent) of a new covenant...*

In the present time the angels join with us in our spiritual war against the kingdom of darkness until God's Kingdom is fully established on the earth. Like the angels, the devil's demons are also active. So it is imperative that we, as the Body of Christ, gain insight and understanding concerning the power and authority given to us by Jesus Christ. Knowing that God always has the enemy outnumbered, but also knowing who we are "in Christ Jesus".

The book of Ephesians chapter 1 and 2, tells us that, *We are seated with Him in Heavenly places in Christ Jesus… "Far above"* all rule and authority and power and dominion and every name that is named. Notice it's not just above, BUT, *"Far above"*. He has given us the authority to negate the devil's ability.

Please remember God always has the upper hand, as we submit to God - He is well able to bring us into complete victory. Luke 10:19 (AMPC) - *Behold! I have given you authority and power to trample upon serpents and scorpions, and [physical and mental strength and ability] over all the power that the enemy [possesses]; and nothing shall in any way harm you.*

So Jesus was declaring, He has given us the authority to negate the devil's ways. We have been given authority over his power to bind and cast down his plans in Jesus' Name!

Jesus said in John 10:10 (AMPC) - *The thief comes only in order to steal and kill and destroy. I came that they may have and enjoy life, and have it in abundance (to the full, till it overflows)*

21

WRAP-UP

As I said at the beginning of the book, our source for understanding angels is the Word of God. I will always test all that I read, learn and hear with the Word of God (the Bible). This is my acid test for truth and understanding in any given subject!

I have opened up the Word of God for us all to learn and be further enlightened on the reality of angels, their existence, and their significant roles in our lives today and every day.

Hopefully, this book will help us all to be equipped with a greater clarity on the subject matter, and to remind us of the angelic resources we have available to us—knowing we can use and activate angels on our behalf and release them on assignments through our prayers to our Heavenly Father. We have a fresh knowledge and understanding of the angelic realm, and now know that we can begin to engage in the supernatural realm and to actively participate in the battle we are all part of!

It tells us in Ephesians 6:12 (AMPC) - *For we are not wrestling with flesh and blood [contending only with physical opponents], but against the despotisms, against the powers, against [the master spirits who are] the world rulers of this present darkness, against the spirit forces of wickedness in the heavenly (supernatural) sphere.*

And hopefully, I have managed to demystify the subject of angels for you and bring understanding to this often-mysterious area of the Bible! Equipping you to know, and given you an understanding that the unseen realm does exist and that it is actually far more real than what we know as reality!!! I have given you some solid Biblical guidelines for understanding the many roles angels play in the world and in the lives of believers.

22

CONCLUSION

It is absolutely essential that we set our minds on the Lord Jesus. It is important that we discipline ourselves to set our minds on thinking and meditating on the things of God, on His precious Word, and on hearing His direction for our lives.

Reminder: Colossians 1:16-17 (AMPC) - *For by Him all things were created in heaven and on earth, [things] visible and invisible, whether thrones or dominions or rulers or authorities; all things were created and exist through Him [that is, by His activity] and for Him. And He Himself existed and is before all things, and in Him all things hold together. [His is the controlling, cohesive force of the universe.]*

2 Corinthians 4:18 (AMPC) - *Since we consider and look not to the things that are seen but to the things that are unseen; for the things that are visible are temporal (brief and fleeting), but the things that are invisible are deathless and everlasting.*

Romans 11:36 (AMPC) - *For from Him and through Him and to Him are all things. [For all things originate with Him and come from Him; all things live through Him and all things center in and tend to consummate and to end in Him.] To Him be the glory forever! Amen*

23

PRAYER AND PRAYER OF SALVATION

I want to take a few moments now to allow each of us to do business with God. I encourage you that He is waiting 24/7 for you to talk to Him, no appointment needed.

The most important decision you can ever make in life is to receive Jesus Christ as Lord and Savior. You can take that life changing step by simply praying the following prayer aloud:

Lord Jesus, I ask You to forgive me of my sins and cleanse me from those things that have kept me in bondage. I surrender to You today. I ask You to come into my heart and be my Lord and Savior. I believe that You are the Son of God and that You were raised from the dead. Thank You for giving me new life as a child of God… In Jesus' name, Amen. **And Amen!**

Leah Leaman
Xtreme Glory Ministries

Ministry Details
Xtreme Glory Ministries
United States of America
Author: Leah Leaman
Email: leahleaman67@gmail.com
www.xtremeglory.co.uk
www.xtremeglory.net

ABOUT THE AUTHOR

Leah Leaman has a passion to encourage people
through the Truth of God's Word. Her hope is to
bring revelation and greater clarity of scriptures from
the Bible to others. Leah has been a Christian for
over 39 years, and lives in California with her family.

Made in the USA
Monee, IL
20 January 2020